# Battles of the War of 1812

**Diane Smolinski**
**and Henry Smolinski**

**Series Consultant:**
**Lieutenant Colonel G.A. LoFaro**

Heinemann Library
Chicago, Illinois

© 2003 Reed Educational & Professional Publishing
Published by Heinemann Library,
an imprint of Reed Educational & Professional
Publishing, Chicago, Illinois

Customer Service  888-454-2279

Visit our website at www.heinemannlibrary.com

Designed by Herman Adler Design
Photo research by Julie Laffin
Printed and bound in the United States by Lake Book
Manufacturing, Inc.

07 06 05 04 03
10 9 8 7 6 5 4 3 2 1

**Library of Congress Cataloging-in-Publication Data**
Smolinski, Diane, 1950-
  Battles of the War of 1812 / Diane Smolinski, Henry
Smolinski.
      p. cm. -- (Americans at war. The War of 1812)
Includes bibliographical references and index.
  ISBN 1-4034-0171-3
  1.  United States--History--War of 1812--Campaigns--
Juvenile literature. [1. United States--History--War of
1812--Campaigns.]  I. Smolinski, Henry. II. Title.
  E355 .S66 2002
  973.5'23--dc21
                                        2002005083

**Acknowledgments**
The authors and publishers are grateful to the following
for permission to reproduce copyright material:
Contents page, pp. 13, 14, 16, 17, 18, 19B, 25, 28
The Granger Collection, New York; p. 4 Smithsonian
Institution; pp. 5, 10, 15, 19T, 26, 27, 29 North Wind
Picture Archives; pp. 7, 11 Bettmann/Corbis; p. 8
United States Senate Historical Office; p.12 National
Archives of Canada; p. 21 Mary Evans Picture Library;
p. 22 Ed Elvidge/Horseshoe Bend Military Park; p. 23
Brown Brothers.

Cover photographs: (main) The Granger Collection,
New York, (border, T-B) Corbis.

**About the Authors**
Diane Smolinski is the author of two previous series of
books on the Revolutionary and Civil Wars. She earned
degrees in education from Duquesne and Slippery Rock
Universities and taught in public schools for 28 years.
Diane now writes for teachers, helping them to use
nonfiction books in their classrooms. Henry Smolinski
served in the U.S. Army and U.S. Army Reserves. He
earned a B.A. from Duquesne University and has
previously contributed ideas and research for a series
of books on the Revolutionary War for young readers.
Diane and Henry currently live in Florida with their
cat, Pepper.

Special thanks to Mike Carpenter for his continuing
encouragement and belief in our abilities to convey a
meaningful message to young readers.

**About the Consultant**
G.A. LoFaro is a lieutenant colonel in the U.S. Army
currently stationed at Fort McPherson, Georgia. After
graduating from West Point, he was commissioned in
the infantry. He has served in a variety of positions in
the 82nd Airborne Division, the Ranger Training
Brigade, and Second Infantry Division in Korea. He
has a Masters Degree in U.S. History from the
University of Michigan and is completing his Ph.D in
U.S. History at the State University of New York at
Stony Brook. He has also served six years on the West
Point faculty where he taught military history to cadets.

On the cover: This colored engraving depicts Thomas Macdonough's victory at the Battle of Lake Champlain in New York on September 11, 1814.
On the contents page: This painting shows the engagement between the USS *Chesapeake* and the HMS *Shannon* off Boston Light on June 1, 1813.

**Note to the Reader**
• The terms North American Indian, Indian, Indian Nation, or the specific tribe names are used here instead of Native
  American. These terms are historically accurate for the time period covered in this book.
• Casualties were not always reported during the War of 1812. Sources sometimes state different casualties for the same
  battles or none at all. In these cases, casualty numbers in the After Action Reports simply state, "unknown."

Some words are shown in bold, **like this.**
You can find out what they mean by looking in the glossary.

# Contents

# Introduction

**From 1775 to 1783, American colonists fought for freedom from British rule. This conflict was called the Revolutionary War, or the War of Independence. In 1812, problems again arose between the new United States and Great Britain.**

People living in the **Northwest Territory** accused the British of giving aid to Indians who were raiding property and attacking settlers. People in New England were outraged that the British were capturing U.S. **merchant** ships, taking **cargo,** and kidnapping U.S. sailors. Attempts to solve these and other differences by passing laws failed.

Upset Americans wanted the United States **Congress** to declare war against Great Britain. The War of 1812, also known as the Second War of Independence, would again find the United States fighting the British over international rights.

## Territory Report

- Thomas Jefferson was the president of the United States throughout many of the events leading up to the War of 1812. James Madison was elected president of the United States in 1809, and signed the declaration of war.

- The King of England at this time was George III (1760–1820).

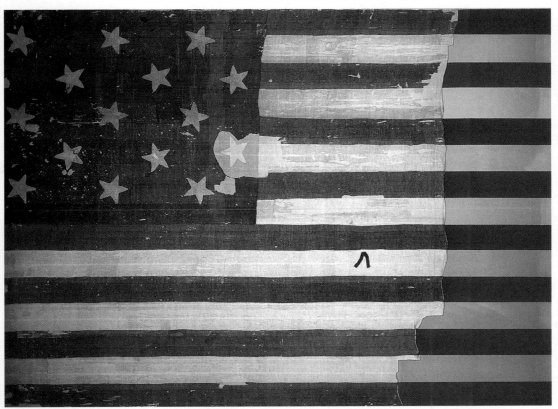

*The United States had flown this flag as an independent nation for only 29 years before Great Britain again tried to control the land and people of North America to satisfy their* **economic** *needs.*

*To keep U.S. merchants from trading with France, the British Navy **blockaded** the east coast of the United States. The much smaller U.S. Navy was not able to stop the British from blockading the coastline.*

## The Embargo Act

Trading with Great Britain was important to the U.S. economy. President Jefferson wanted merchants to stop trading with Great Britain until they agreed to stop raiding U.S. ships. In December 1807, Congress passed a law called the Embargo Act. This law made it illegal for all U.S. **vessels** to sail for foreign ports. In 1807, the U.S. **exported** $108 million worth of goods. In 1808, they only exported $22 million worth of goods. This created a great hardship for merchants who depended on trade to earn a living.

## More Laws

In 1809, Congress **repealed** the Embargo Act and passed another law that allowed merchants to trade with all countries except Great Britain and France. This did not solve the merchants' money problems though, since Great Britain and France were the United States' biggest trading partners. Once U.S. merchant ships started to sail to other countries, Great Britain continued to attack their ships.

## Territory Report

The British Navy, also called the Royal Navy, was much larger than the U.S. Navy at this time. At the start of the War of 1812, the U.S. Navy had less than 40 vessels. Even though most of its ships were fighting a war in Europe, the British Navy had more than 600 ships.

## The Northwest Territory

In 1812, the present-day states of Ohio, Michigan, Indiana, Wisconsin, and Illinois were called the **Northwest Territory.** American pioneers were moving west to settle these lands. Indians wanted to keep these lands for themselves, using them for hunting and fishing as their ancestors had done. They attacked the settlers to protect this property.

The British promised the Indians that they could keep their lands if they would continue trading furs with them and keep the settlers away. Once the war started, this promise made Indians more willing to fight on the side of the British.

### Territory Report

#### U.S. Territories Earn Their Statehood

When the War of 1812 began, only Ohio was a state. The other parts of the Northwest Territory were still considered territories. The dates below indicate when the territories became states.

| | |
|---|---|
| Ohio | March 1, 1803 |
| Indiana | December 11, 1816 |
| Illinois | December 3, 1818 |
| Michigan | January 26, 1837 |
| Wisconsin | May 29, 1848 |

The region known as the Northwest Territory contained valuable natural resources such as furs, timber, and minerals like iron and coal. The British wanted access to these natural resources for **export** back home.

*James Madison (left) served as Secretary of State while Thomas Jefferson (right) was president. James Madison was then elected president of the United States from 1809–1817.*

## Moving Closer to War

As part of the peace settlement to end the **Revolutionary War,** Great Britain agreed to leave U.S. territory and move into Canada. They did not keep this promise.

The settlers in the Northwest Territory asked **Congress** and President Jefferson to force the British to leave this territory. They wanted the United States to invade Canada. Americans thought the British would return to Canada to defend their **colony** and leave the Indians alone to deal with **westward expansion.**

### Territory Report

In the Northeastern United States, citizens were more hesitant to go to war with Great Britain because Great Britain was a valuable trading partner.

## A New Leader

President Jefferson was not able to resolve the problems between the United States and Great Britain while he was president. In 1809, voters in the United States elected a new president, James Madison. Madison would now need to lead the nation in this time of crisis.

# The War of 1812 Begins

## Declaration of War

On June 1, 1812 President James Madison asked the United States **Congress** to declare war against Great Britain. Many members of Congress argued against going to war because the New England **merchants** and shipping community depended on trade with Great Britain to support their businesses.

On June 18, 1812, Congress voted to go to war with Great Britain. While the British were busy fighting France in Europe, the United States planned to capture Canada, a **colony** of Britain. They wanted to invade Canada by way of three **fronts,** the Detroit Frontier, the Niagara Frontier, and Montreal.

*The representatives in Congress from the **Northwest Territory** that favored going to war were called "War Hawks." The representatives in Congress that were against going to war were called "Federalists." George W. Campbell, a senator from Tennessee, was a War Hawk. William Hunter, a senator from Rhode Island, was a Federalist.*

### Territory Report

#### The Vote in Congress

- The U.S. House of Representatives—79 voted for war and 49 voted against war.

- The U.S. Senate—19 voted for war and 13 voted against it.

*William Hunter*

*George W. Campbell*

| 1812 | 1813 |
|---|---|
| **6/18  U.S. declares war on Great Britain** <br> **7/17  U.S. surrenders Fort Mackinac** | |

# Land Battles of 1812

## Fort Mackinac
## July 17, 1812

The British wanted to drive the U.S. from Mackinac Island. All trade routes to the western Great Lakes could be controlled from this small island. The British wanted to use the island as a fur trading post.

### Territory Report

Even though there were a few farms on Mackinac Island, the people who lived there depended on the fur trade for income.

Before the United States could put their plan to invade Canada into action, the British surprised the U.S. soldiers at Fort Mackinac. On July 17, 1812, nearly 150 British **militia** and 280 Ottawa and Chippewa Indians landed on Mackinac Island. They surrounded the fort and positioned a cannon on higher ground overlooking the fort. The 57 Americans inside Fort Mackinac surrendered.

Great Britain won its first victory of the war without firing a shot.

| After Action Report | United States | Great Britain |
| --- | --- | --- |
| Commanders | Lieutenant Porter Hanks | Captain Charles Roberts |
| Casualties | 0 | 0 |
| Outcome | defeat | victory |

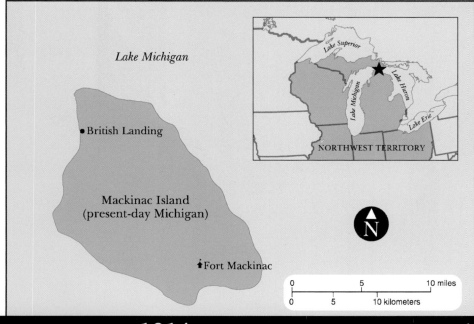

In 1812, Mackinac Island, located between Lakes Huron and Michigan, was the northernmost military post in the United States. The settlement on Mackinac Island included a small U.S. fort, Fort Mackinac.

**1814**          **1815**

## Preparing to Attack Canada

In July of 1812, U.S. General William Hull assembled an army of about 1,500 Ohio **militiamen** and 300 **regulars** in preparation for the invasion of Canada. From Ohio, he marched to Fort Detroit in what is now the state of Michigan. Hull's army then crossed the Detroit River into Canada and stopped to wait for supplies. When supplies did not arrive as expected, Hull withdrew the army to Fort Detroit.

## Fort Dearborn
## August 15, 1812

After the attack on Fort Mackinac, General Hull worried that the British would attack Fort Dearborn next. He sent some of his men to lead the soldiers and civilians living in Fort Dearborn to the safety of Fort Detroit.

### Territory Report

Fort Dearborn was located near the present-day city of Chicago, Illinois. Under the command of Captain Nathan Heald, 65 soldiers and about 25 civilians defended Fort Dearborn.

On August 15, 1812, a group of Indians agreed to help escort the Americans to safety. Once outside Fort Dearborn, these Indians killed most of the soldiers and civilians.

*Fort Dearborn was named after Henry Dearborn, the U.S. Secretary of War from 1801 to 1809.*

### 1812

6/18 U.S. declares war on Great Britain
7/17 U.S. surrenders Fort Mackinac
8/15 U.S. abandons Fort Dearborn
8/16 U.S. surrenders Fort Detroit

### 1813

*For surrendering Fort Detroit without a fight, General Hull was sentenced to death by a U.S. military court for "cowardice and neglect of duty." Even though he was found guilty, President James Madison pardoned him.*

## Fort Detroit
## August 16, 1812

Fort Detroit sat near the Detroit River, a boundary between the United States and Canada. It protected the city of Detroit from enemy invasion.

When General Hull withdrew from Canada back to Fort Detroit, the British followed. British regulars, Canadian soldiers, and Indians crossed the Detroit River and prepared to attack Fort Detroit. General Hull worried that the Indians would **massacre** his troops at Fort Detroit. Before the British began their attack, General Hull surrendered.

## Disappointing First Year

The loss of Forts Mackinac, Dearborn, and Detroit left most of the **Northwest Territory** undefended. The government was in debt trying to build an army. Many men were lost. The war did not go well for the U.S. in the western frontier during this first year.

| After Action Report | United States | Great Britain |
|---|---|---|
| **Commanders** | General William Hull | General Isaac Brock |
| **Casualties** | 0 | 0 |
| **Outcome** | defeat | victory |

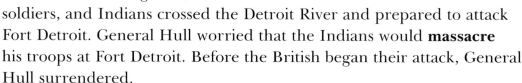

1814         1815

## The Niagara Frontier

On the second **front,** U.S. troops crossed the Niagara River and planned to attack the Canadian town of Queenston. It was located on high ground above the Niagara River.

## Battle of Queenston Heights
## October 13, 1812

The British were positioned on the hills above the Niagara River. U.S. army troops climbed the hills and forced the British to withdraw into the town of Queenston. The Americans waited for reinforcements, but some of the **militia** forces refused to cross the river. British troops from nearby Fort George came to help the British soldiers. Without help from the militia, the Americans were forced to surrender.

The first two invasion attempts ended in disaster for the United States. General Dearborn would now lead the third U.S. force into Canada.

*Boats were used by U.S. Army troops to cross the Niagara River to attack British forces around the city of Queenston.*

### Territory Report

• General Isaac Brock, commander of the British forces, was killed at this battle.

• In an attempt to escape capture by the British, many U.S. soldiers tried to swim across the Niagara River back to the U.S. side. Some soldiers drowned, while others were captured.

| After Action Report | United States | Great Britain |
| --- | --- | --- |
| Commanders | Gen. Stephen Van Rensselaer | Gen. Isaac Brock |
| Casualties | unknown | unknown |
| Outcome | defeat | victory |

**1812**                **1813**

6/18  **U.S. declares war on Great Britain**
7/17  **U.S. surrenders Fort Mackinac**
8/15  **U.S. abandons Fort Dearborn**
8/16  **U.S. surrenders Fort Detroit**
10/13  **Battle of Queenston Heights**

## Montreal
## November 1812

The U.S. would again try to invade Canada. This time, by attacking Montreal.

This attempt did not go as planned. General Henry Dearborn crossed into Canada with **regular** U.S. army troops. Again, the militia refused to cross the border. After a short fight, Dearborn retreated back across the border to the U.S. side. This marked the end of the U.S. invasion of Canada in 1812.

Many Americans felt these failed invasion attempts were largely due to the lack of leadership from U.S. Generals Hull, Van Rensselaer, and Dearborn, and were also due to a lack of direction and strategy from the U.S. War Department.

*Henry Dearborn was a commander in the U.S. Army during the **Revolutionary War** (1775–1783). He then served as a Major General in the U.S. Army during the War of 1812.*

1814

1815

# Naval Battles of 1812

During the War of 1812, the powerful British Navy controlled the open seas. The British were determined to keep the United States from trading with other nations.

## "Old Ironsides"
## August 19, 1812

The USS *Constitution* and the HMS *Guerrière* battled each other in the Atlantic Ocean about 750 miles (1,200 kilometers) east of Boston. The *Guerrière* fired its cannons at the *Constitution* even though the two ships were still a distance apart. Cannonballs bounced off the **hull** of the *Constitution*. American sailors remarked, "her sides are made of iron." This led to the *Constitution's* nickname "Old Ironsides." Once the *Constitution* sailed to within 150 feet (46 meters) of the *Guerrière*, it fired several **broadsides,** destroying the British ship.

The British were shocked that a single U.S. Navy ship could defeat one of their warships.

*Cannons on British warships were mainly designed to fire long distances. The U.S. ships also had some long-distance cannons, but they mainly depended on shorter-range cannons that required them to get closer to an enemy ship before firing.*

## Territory Report
### Ships' Abbreviations

- *HMS* means "His Majesty's Ship."
- *USS* means "United States Ship."

| After Action Report | United States | Great Britain |
| --- | --- | --- |
| **Commanders** | Captain Isaac Hull | Captain James R. Dacres |
| **Casualties** | 9 killed, 11 wounded | 15 killed, 63 wounded |
| **Outcome** | victory | defeat |

| 1812 | 1813 |
| --- | --- |

6/18  U.S. declares war on Great Britain
7/17  U.S. surrenders Fort Mackinac
8/15  U.S. abandons Fort Dearborn
8/16  U.S. surrenders Fort Detroit
8/19  USS *Constitution* defeats the HMS *Guerrière*
10/13  Battle of Queenston Heights

Most privateers were owned by businessmen or wealthy merchants only interested in making money. The men who sailed these ships were also called privateers. During the first six months of the war, privateers captured over 450 British merchant ships.

## Privateers

Victories by U.S. Navy ships in 1812 were important, but they were not enough to stop the British Navy from interfering with U.S. trade. Citizens thought that **privateers** could help disrupt British **merchant** shipping.

Privateers were small, fast warships that mainly sailed along the east coast of North America and in the **West Indies.** They attacked British merchant ships not protected by the British Navy and took their **cargo.** The British Navy was unable to stop them. Even though the privateers inconvenienced the British, they did not affect the outcome of the war.

**Congress** now needed money to continue the war. The U.S. Navy victories during 1812 helped members of Congress to convince Americans to support the war.

## Territory Report

At the end of 1812, both the U.S. and Great Britain suffered unexpected setbacks.

- On land, the U.S. did not defeat the British Army in Canada.

- At sea, the British were embarrassed by the ability of the U.S. Navy to defeat some of their ships.

1814          1815

# Land Battles of 1813

As the second year of the war began, the U.S. Army was more prepared. **Congress** approved better pay for soldiers and authorized the size of the **Regular** Army to be increased to 30,000 men. Recently fought battles produced more experienced soldiers. The U.S. was still determined to invade Canada.

### Raisin River Massacre
### January 23, 1813

In January of 1813, a group of 1,000 Kentucky Volunteers clashed with Canadian **militia**, British Regulars, and Indians in a U.S. settlement called Frenchtown on the Raisin River. The volunteers easily defeated the militia.

Upon hearing the news, the British sent soldiers from Fort Detroit to recapture this settlement. The U.S. volunteers surrendered after a short, fierce fight. The British promised to treat the U.S. prisoners fairly, but did not keep their word. Healthy prisoners were taken to Fort Detroit. Wounded prisoners were left behind. That night, Indians **massacred** the wounded prisoners.

*Frenchtown was a small settlement about twenty miles (32 kilometers) south of Detroit. At this time, the British controlled the city of Detroit, after taking it from General Hull in 1812.*

| After Action Report | United States | Great Britain |
|---|---|---|
| Commanders | General James Winchester | General Henry Procter |
| Casualties | 100 killed, 500 captured | unknown |
| Outcome | defeat | victory |

| 1812 | 1813 |
|---|---|
| 6/18 U.S. declares war on Great Britain | 1/23 Raisin River Massacre |
| 7/17 U.S. surrenders Fort Mackinac | 10/5 Battle of the Thames |
| 8/15 U.S. abandons Fort Dearborn | |
| 8/16 U.S. surrenders Fort Detroit | |
| 8/19 USS *Constitution* defeats the HMS *Guerrière* | |
| 10/13 Battle of Queenston Heights | |

## Battle of the Thames
## October 5, 1813

U.S. troops were angry over the mistreatment of American prisoners at Raisin River.

Marching to invade Canada, another group of Kentucky Volunteers met British Army troops and a group of Shawnee Indians along the Thames River, in Canada. Preparing to defend themselves, British troops formed a **battle line.** U.S. troops charged and broke through the line on horseback. The Shawnee Indian Chief, Tecumseh, was killed. With their leader dead, the Shawnee abandoned the battlefield. The U.S. Army achieved a complete victory.

*Tecumseh fought on the side of Great Britain during the War of 1812, hoping that when the British won the war they would return lands to his people.*

## A Turning Point

By winning the Battle of the Thames, the U.S. again controlled much of the **Northwest Territory.** The Indians no longer had a strong leader who could unite the Indian Nations.

At this same time, the U.S. Navy was battling for control of the Great Lakes.

### After Action Report

|  | United States | Great Britain | Indian |
|---|---|---|---|
| **Commanders** | General William H. Harrison | General Henry Procter | Tecumseh |
| **Casualties** | 7 killed, 22 wounded | 12 killed, 22 wounded | 35 killed, 477 prisoners |
| **Outcome** | victory | defeat | defeat |

1814      1815

# Naval Battles of 1813

## Perry takes Command

In the spring of 1813, Commodore Oliver H. Perry was given command of the U.S. fleet on Lake Erie. His fleet consisted of five ships, including a **converted merchant** ship and four new ships still under construction. Perry's ships were finally ready to sail in August of 1813.

Before he could sail, Perry needed to find sailors to man his ships. The commander of the entire Great Lakes Fleet transferred some sailors to Perry's ships. U.S. Army General William Henry Harrison also sent about 100 Kentucky Riflemen to work on the ships.

In September of 1813, Commodore Perry sailed his fleet into the western part of Lake Erie in search of the British.

*Commodore Perry (right) named his **flagship** the* Lawrence, *after his friend Captain James Lawrence who was killed in a naval battle during this war.*

### Territory Report

#### Fleets at Lake Erie

| Great Britain | United States |
| --- | --- |
| *Detroit*–19 guns | *Lawrence*–20 guns |
| *Queen Charlotte*–17 guns | *Niagara*–20 guns |
| *Brig-Hunter*–13 guns | *Ariel*–6 guns |
| *Lady Prevost*–10 guns | *Caledonia*–3 guns |
| *Chippoway*–1 gun | *Somers*–2 guns |
| *Little Belt*–1 gun | *Scorpion*–1 gun |
| | *Porcupine*–1 gun |
| | *Tigress*–1 gun |
| | *Trippe*–1 gun |

---

| 1812 | 1813 |
| --- | --- |
| 6/18 U.S. declares war on Great Britain | 1/23 Raisin River Massacre |
| 7/17 U.S. surrenders Fort Mackinac | 9/10 Battle of Lake Erie |
| 8/15 U.S. abandons Fort Dearborn | 10/5 Battle of the Thames |
| 8/16 U.S. surrenders Fort Detroit | |
| 8/19 USS *Constitution* defeats the HMS *Guerrière* | |
| 10/13 Battle of Queenston Heights | |

## The Battle of Lake Erie
### September 10, 1813

When the British fleet was located, Commodore Perry commanded his men to sail the USS *Lawrence* toward them. Two other U.S. ships followed. The British ships fired and did much damage to the three American ships. After two hours of fighting, nearly all of Perry's men aboard the *Lawrence* were killed or wounded.

Refusing to surrender, Commodore Perry and a few of his men rowed a small boat back to one of the U.S. ships that stayed behind, the USS *Niagara*. They sailed the *Niagara* into battle against the two largest British ships. Already damaged from battle with the *Lawrence*, the British ships surrendered. The other ships of Perry's fleet then captured the remaining ships of the British fleet.

The U.S. now controlled the Great Lakes.

*Commodore Perry is best known for rowing from the* Lawrence *to the* Niagara *in order to defeat the British at the Battle of Lake Erie.*

*Commodore Perry wrote this note after his victory at the Battle of Lake Erie. It begins, "We have met the enemy and they are ours."*

We have met the enemy and they are ours. Two Ships, two Brigs one Schooner & one Sloop.
Yours, with great respect and esteem
O.H. Perry.

| After Action Report | United States | Great Britain |
| --- | --- | --- |
| Commanders | Commodore Oliver Perry | Captain Robert H. Garclay |
| Casualties | 27 killed, 93 wounded | 41 killed, 91 wounded |
| Outcome | victory | defeat |

1814

1815

## Blockade of the East Coast

The British Navy **blockaded** the east coast of the United States, keeping U.S. **merchants** from shipping their goods by ocean routes. Transporting goods such as sugar, flour, and rice over inland roads was slow and expensive. This created shortages and caused high prices in many U.S. cities.

The British blockade forced U.S. Navy ships to remain in U.S. ports where they could be protected by **shore batteries.** With so few ships in the navy, Americans could not take a chance on trying to break through the blockade. The U.S. Navy could do very little to stop British ships from raiding coastal communities.

*The British blockade of the east coast of the United States extended from Charleston, South Carolina, to Delaware Bay in New England.*

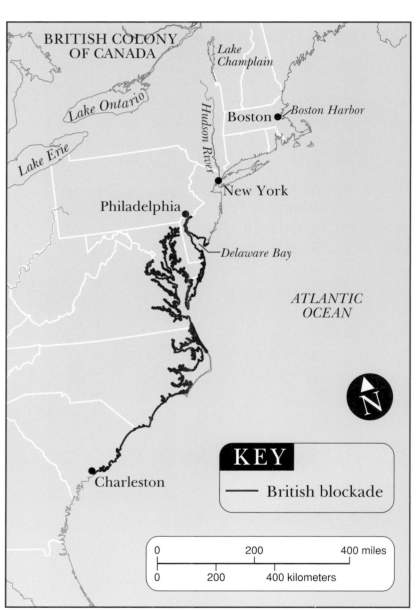

## Territory Report

### British Blockade

In early 1813, the British blockade consisted of:

- 10 ships of the line (large warships)
- 38 **frigates**
- 52 smaller **vessels**

| 1812 | 1813 |
|---|---|
| 6/18 U.S. declares war on Great Britain | 1/23 Raisin River Massacre |
| 7/17 U.S. surrenders Fort Mackinac | 6/1 USS *Chesapeake* battles the HMS *Shannon* |
| 8/15 U.S. abandons Fort Dearborn | 9/10 Battle of Lake Erie |
| 8/16 U.S. surrenders Fort Detroit | 10/5 Battle of the Thames |
| 8/19 USS *Constitution* defeats the HMS *Guerrière* | |
| 10/13 Battle of Queenston Heights | |

### The USS *Chesapeake* Battles the HMS *Shannon* June 1, 1813

Even though the USS *Chesapeake* was blockaded in Boston Harbor, the British commander of the HMS *Shannon* challenged it to a one-on-one battle.

On June 1, 1813, Captain James Lawrence sailed the *Chesapeake* from Boston Harbor to fight the British frigate, the *Shannon*. The two ships met and fired **broadsides** at close range for about half an hour. The British crew was better trained and caused much damage to the *Chesapeake*. Wounded, Captain Lawrence urged his men to continue the battle by saying, "Don't give up the ship." The *Chesapeake* was unable to sail and was captured by the British.

The U.S. Navy had little success fighting the British on the Atlantic Ocean in 1813.

*Captain James Lawrence's words, "Don't give up the ship," became the motto of the United States Navy.*

## Territory Report

After the battle, the British moved the USS *Chesapeake* to Halifax, Nova Scotia, and then to England.

| After Action Report | United States | Great Britain |
| --- | --- | --- |
| Commanders | Captain James Lawrence | Captain Philip Broke |
| Casualties | 47 killed, 99 wounded | 27 killed, 59 wounded |
| Outcome | defeat | victory |

1814      1815

# Battles of 1814–1815

## The Chesapeake Bay

For now, the United States continued to win battles on the Western and Southern frontiers. General Andrew Jackson defeated the Creek Indians in a series of battles in the territory that is now Alabama. The Creek Indian Nation was defeated at the Battle of Horseshoe Bend and signed a treaty giving up claim to twenty million acres (eight million hectares) of land.

## War Ends in Europe

After Great Britain finished fighting the war in Europe, they sent ships and soldiers to North America to fight in the War of 1812. They planned to attack the U.S. on three **fronts.**

*On March 27–28, 1814, about 2,000 **militiamen,** 600 U.S. **Regular** Army soldiers, and several hundred Indians friendly to the U.S. Army, fought about 1,000 Creek Indians at a place called Horseshoe Bend in what is now Alabama.*

### Territory Report

#### British Plan of Attack

- One force would sail into the Chesapeake Bay.

- A second force in the Niagara Frontier would sail across Lake Champlain and down the Hudson River.

- A third force would capture New Orleans at the mouth of the Mississippi River.

| 1812 | 1813 |
|---|---|
| 6/18 U.S. declares war on Great Britain | 1/23 Raisin River Massacre |
| 7/17 U.S. surrenders Fort Mackinac | 6/1 USS *Chesapeake* battles the HMS *Shannon* |
| 8/15 U.S. abandons Fort Dearborn | 9/10 Battle of Lake Erie |
| 8/16 U.S. surrenders Fort Detroit | 10/5 Battle of the Thames |
| 8/19 USS *Constitution* defeats the HMS *Guerrière* | |
| 10/13 Battle of Queenston Heights | |

*At dawn on September 14, 1814, Francis Scott Key saw the American flag flying over Fort McHenry and wrote a poem about what he saw. This poem, "The Star Spangled Banner," became our National Anthem.*

## Attack on Washington, D.C.
## August 25, 1814

The British began their **offensive** near Washington D.C., the capital city of the United States. They landed in Chesapeake Bay and marched to Washington D.C., burning many buildings there, including the White House and the **Capitol.** British troops then returned to their ships and set sail for Baltimore.

## Attack on Baltimore, Maryland
## September 13–14, 1814

British ships carrying about 4,500 British soldiers landed near Baltimore. As they marched toward the city, a force of U.S. soldiers and militia stopped the invasion attempt. The British decided not to attack and returned to their ships.

## Attack on Fort McHenry
## September 13–14, 1814

At the same time British forces marched toward Baltimore, the British Navy bombarded Fort McHenry. Firing from such a great distance, few shells hit the U.S. fort. The Americans refused to give up. Not wanting to risk sailing closer to and being hit by U.S. cannons, the British left the harbor. The British left Chesapeake Bay without the victory they wanted.

| After Action Report | United States | Great Britain |
|---|---|---|
| Commanders | Major George Armistead (commander of Fort McHenry) | Admiral Alexander Cochrane (commander of the British fleet) General Robert Ross (commander of the land forces, killed during this battle) |
| Casualties | 4 killed, 24 wounded | unknown |
| Outcome | victory | defeat |

**1814**                    **1815**

3/27–28  Battle of Horseshoe Bend
8/25  Attack and burning of Washington, D.C.
9/13–14  Attack on Baltimore, MD and Fort McHenry

## The Niagara Region
### August 31, 1814

The British began the second part of their invasion of the United States in the Niagara Region. They wanted to cut New England into two parts.

## Battle of Plattsburgh
### September 11, 1814

More than 10,000 British soldiers began the march from Canada. Small parties of U.S. **militia** were sent to slow down the British advance. The nearly 3,400 U.S. militiamen in Plattsburgh, New York, were not able to stop the British. So, they retreated south of the city and across the Saranac River. When the British reached Plattsburgh, they did not follow the U.S. militia. They decided to wait for help from the British fleet before crossing the Saranac River.

While British land troops waited in Plattsburgh, the British Navy decided to attack the U.S. ships that were anchored in nearby Plattsburgh Bay.

*The British marched from Canada along Lake Champlain and down the Hudson River to New York City.*

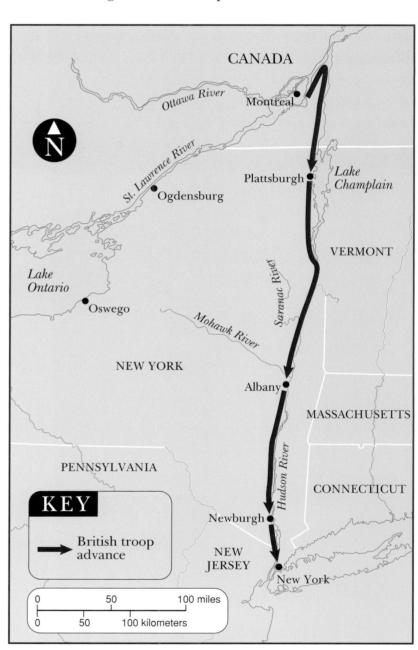

| 1812 | 1813 |
|---|---|
| 6/18  U.S. declares war on Great Britain | 1/23  Raisin River Massacre |
| 7/17  U.S. surrenders Fort Mackinac | 6/1  USS *Chesapeake* battles the HMS *Shannon* |
| 8/15  U.S. abandons Fort Dearborn | 9/10  Battle of Lake Erie |
| 8/16  U.S. surrenders Fort Detroit | 10/5  Battle of the Thames |
| 8/19  USS *Constitution* defeats the HMS *Guerrière* | |
| 10/13  Battle of Queenston Heights | |

## The Battle of Lake Champlain
### September 11, 1814

As the British ships sailed into the bay, they opened fire on the U.S. ships. A furious battle began that lasted two hours. Both U.S. and British ships suffered serious damage from **broadsides** fired at close range. In the end, the U.S. **maneuvered** their ships to force the British to surrender.

*Even though the battle is known as the Battle of Lake Champlain, it was fought in Plattsburgh Bay, which is part of Lake Champlain.*

| After Action Report—Battle of Lake Champlain | United States | Great Britain |
|---|---|---|
| Commanders | Lieutenant Thomas Macdonough | Captain George Downie |
| Casualties | 52 killed, 58 wounded | 84 killed, 110 wounded |
| Outcome | victory | defeat |

## The End of the Battle of Plattsburgh
### September 11, 1814

Once the naval battle began on Lake Champlain, British land troops decided to cross the Saranac River and attack the U.S. militia. The inexperienced U.S. militia was no match for the **veteran** British troops. Complete defeat for the U.S. seemed certain. However, learning that the British fleet had been defeated on Lake Champlain, British General Prevost ordered a retreat.

These U.S. victories upset British political leaders in Canada and England. With peace **negotiations** in progress, they now wanted to end the fighting.

| After Action Report—Battle of Plattsburgh | United States | Great Britain |
|---|---|---|
| Commanders | Gen. Alexander Macomb | Gen. George Prevost |
| Casualties | unknown | unknown |
| Outcome | victory | defeat |

**1814**

**1815**

3/27–28 **Battle of Horseshoe Bend**
8/25 **Attack and burning of Washington, D.C.**
9/11 **Battle of Lake Champlain**
9/11 **Battle of Plattsburgh**
9/13–14 **Attack on Baltimore, MD and Fort McHenry**

## New Orleans

The final part of the British plan to invade the United States involved capturing the city of New Orleans. By controlling the entrance to the Mississippi River, they could move goods and supplies to and from the center of the United States to markets around the world.

## Preparing for Battle

U.S. troops prepared for the British attack on New Orleans by building a **defensive** line of logs and dirt outside the city. Before reaching the city, the British would have to find their way through surrounding swamps. Local fishermen guided British soldiers through these swamps. The U.S. troops were surprised when the British arrived near the city.

## The Battle Begins

While British troops rested from their march, the U.S. attacked. The battle was fought to a draw.

*Both armies had to be careful not to march into swampy land whenever fog rolled in or the tides changed. Many dangerous animals, including alligators, lived in these swamps.*

| 1812 | 1813 |
|---|---|
| 6/18 U.S. declares war on Great Britain | 1/23 Raisin River Massacre |
| 7/17 U.S. surrenders Fort Mackinac | 6/1 USS *Chesapeake* battles the HMS *Shannon* |
| 8/15 U.S. abandons Fort Dearborn | 9/10 Battle of Lake Erie |
| 8/16 U.S. surrenders Fort Detroit | 10/5 Battle of the Thames |
| 8/19 USS *Constitution* defeats the HMS *Guerrière* | |
| 10/13 Battle of Queenston Heights | |

## Battle of New Orleans
## January 8, 1815

Both sides withdrew. The British waited for more soldiers. The U.S. extended and strengthened their defensive wall around New Orleans. They knew the British would soon be ready to renew the fight.

**Territory Report**

This battle had no affect on the outcome of the war. The U.S. and Great Britain agreed to a peace settlement on December 24, 1814.

## The Battle is Decided

The British started their attack on the morning of January 8, 1815. British troops sent to distract the U.S. troops got lost. This caused the attack to start later than planned. The early morning fog began to disappear and did not provide the cover that the British had planned. When British troops crossed an open field to attack the waiting U.S. troops, their colorful uniforms made perfect shooting targets. The British charged several times, but each time they were turned back by the cannon and rifle fire of the Americans.

| After Action Report | United States | Great Britain |
| --- | --- | --- |
| **Commanders** | General Andrew Jackson | General Edward Pakenham (killed during this battle) |
| **Casualties** | 50 killed, 200 wounded, 100 missing or captured | 400 killed, 1,500 wounded, 550 missing or captured |
| **Outcome** | victory | defeat |

Retreating to their original positions, the British left the area after a few days.

*U.S. General Andrew Jackson (on horseback) organized army troops,* **militia,** *and volunteers into a defensive force around the city of New Orleans.*

| 1814 | 1815 |
| --- | --- |
| **3/27–28  Battle of Horseshoe Bend**<br>**8/25  Attack and burning of Washington, D.C.**<br>**9/11  Battle of Lake Champlain**<br>**9/11  Battle of Plattsburgh**<br>**9/13–14  Attack on Baltimore, MD and Fort McHenry** | **1/8  Battle of New Orleans** |

# The Treaty of Ghent

**Even though the war had not ended, peace negotiations began in August of 1814 in the city of Ghent, Belgium.**

On December 24, 1814, after almost six months of negotiations, Great Britain and the United States agreed to a settlement. The Treaty contains eleven articles, explaining in detail many of the conditions of *Article I:*

### Article 1

*There shall be a ... peace between His Britannic Majesty and the United States, ... All hostilities, both by sea and land, shall cease as soon as this treaty shall have been ratified by both parties, ... All territory, ... taken by either party from the other during the war, ... shall be restored without delay, ...*

*Sweden was originally chosen as the site for peace negotiations. When the war in Europe ended, Belgium was chosen instead because it was closer in distance to travel for both countries.*

## Territory Report

### Treaty Delegates

**United States:**
John Quincy Adams
James A. Bayard
Henry Clay
Jonathan Russell
Albert Gallatin

**Great Britain:**
Right Honourable James Lord Gambier
Henry Goulburn
William Adams

## 1812

6/18  U.S. declares war on Great Britain
7/17  U.S. surrenders Fort Mackinac
8/15  U.S. abandons Fort Dearborn
8/16  U.S. surrenders Fort Detroit
8/19  USS *Constitution* defeats the HMS *Guerrière*
10/13  Battle of Queenston Heights

## 1813

1/23  Raisin River Massacre
6/1  USS *Chesapeake* battles the HMS *Shannon*
9/10  Battle of Lake Erie
10/5  Battle of the Thames

# After the War

**The Treaty of Ghent stopped the fighting, but it did not solve the problems that led to the War of 1812. The U.S. demand that Great Britain stop illegally searching U.S. ships and kidnapping U.S. sailors was not mentioned.**

Even though *Article IX* of the Treaty stated that both nations would:

*… end, … hostilities with all the tribes or nations of Indians … and to restore … all the possessions, rights, and privileges which they may have … been entitled to in one thousand eight hundred and eleven,…*

Indians were forced from their lands as the United States began to expand westward.

Since travel by ship across the Atlantic Ocean from Europe to North America was slow, word of peace did not reach the U.S. until February 11, 1815. On February 15, 1815, **Congress** approved the Treaty of Ghent. The War of 1812 was officially over.

*It took almost two months for the Treaty of Ghent to reach the U.S. from Belgium. During that time, the U.S. had no way of knowing if peace had been reached.*

**Evening Gazette Office,**

Boston, Monday, 10, A.M.

The following most highly important handbill has just been issued from the Centinel press. We deem it a duty that we owe our Friends and the Public to assist in the prompt spread of the Glorious News.

## Treaty of PEACE signed and arrived.

*Centinel Office, Feb. 13, 1815, 8 o'clock in the morning.*

WE have this instant received in Thirty-two hours from New-York the following

## Great and Happy News!

FOR THE PUBLIC.

To BENJAMIN RUSSELL, Esq. Centinel-Office, Boston.

New-York, Feb. 11, 1815—Saturday Evening, 10 o'clock.

SIR—

I HASTEN to acquaint you, for the information of the Public, of the arrival here this afternoon of H. Br. M. sloop of war *Favorite*, in which has come passenger Mr CARROLL American Messenger, having in his possession

## A Treaty of Peace

Between this Country and Great-Britain, signed on the 26th December last.

Mr Baker also is on board, as Agent for the British Government, the same who was formerly Charge des Affairs here.

Mr Carroll reached town at eight o'clock this evening. He shewed to a friend of mine, who is acquainted with him, the pacquet containing the Treaty, and a London newspaper of the last date of December, announcing the signing of the Treaty.

It depends, however, as my friend observed, upon the act of the President to suspend hostilities on this side.

The gentleman left London the 2d Jan. The Transit had sailed previously from a port on the Continent.

This city is in a perfect uproar of joy, shouts, illuminations, &c. &c.

I have undertaken to send you this by Express—the rider engaging to deliver it by Eight o'clock on Monday morning. The expense will be 225 dollars :—If you can collect so much to indemnify me I will thank you to do so.

I am with respect, Sir, your obedient servant,

————— JONATHAN GOODHUE.

☞ We most heartily, felicitate our Country on this auspicious news, which may be relied on as wholly authentic.—CENTINEL.

PEACE EXTRA.

| 1814 | 1815 |
| --- | --- |
| **3/27–28 Battle of Horseshoe Bend** | **1/8 Battle of New Orleans** |
| **8/25 Attack and burning of Washington, D.C.** | **2/15 Congress approves the Treaty of Ghent** |
| **9/11 Battle of Lake Champlain** | |
| **9/11 Battle of Plattsburgh** | |
| **9/13–14 Attack on Baltimore, MD and Fort McHenry** | |

# Glossary

**battle line**   straight line of men standing shoulder to shoulder

**blockade**   troops or warships that block enemy troops or supplies from entering or leaving an area

**broadside**   firing all the cannons mounted on one side of a ship at the same time

**Capitol**   building in which the U.S. Congress meets in Washington, D.C.

**cargo**   goods carried by a ship for trading

**colony**   territory settled by people from other countries who still had loyalty to those other countries. The word *colonist* is used to describe a person who lives in a colony.

**Congress**   men who represented the individual states in the U.S. government, either in the House of Representatives or the Senate

**convert**   to change from one type of thing, like a ship, to another

**defensive**   protection against attack

**economy**   how money is earned and spent and how goods and services are produced and sold

**export**   to ship goods and materials to another country

**flagship**   ship that the leader of a group of ships sails on

**frigate**   type of sailing warship that was designed to go fast

**front**   place where fighting is happening between enemy forces

**hull**   sides of a ship

**maneuver**   to move to a planned position

**massacre**   to murder

**merchant**   ship that carries goods for trading, or a person who buys and sells goods

**militia**   small military unit of ordinary men organized by an individual state. Men who fought in a militia were called *militiamen*.

**negotiation**   talk between two or more people or groups to work out an agreement

**Northwest Territory**   land that covered the present-day states of Ohio, Michigan, Illinois, Indiana, and Wisconsin

**offensive**   attack

**privateer**   small, fast warship used to disrupt British merchant shipping. The men who sailed on these ships were also known as privateers.

**regular**   full-time soldier

**repeal**   to officially cancel

**Revolutionary War**   American fight for independence from British rule between 1775–1783

**shore battery**   group of cannons near the water used to protect a city or harbor

**vessel**   boat

**veteran**   experienced

**West Indies**   group of islands between North and South America

**westward expansion**   movement of settlers from the eastern United States to less populated lands to the west

# Historical Fiction to Read

Buckey, Sarah Masters. *The Smuggler's Treasure (American Girl History Mysteries Series #1)*.
Middleton, Wis.: Pleasant Company, 1999.
In New Orleans during the War of 1812, an eleven-year-old girl is determined to find a
pirate's treasure to use as ransom for her imprisoned father.

Gillem, Harriette and Robinet Gillem. *Washington City is Burning*. New York: Simon and
Schuster, 1996.
A slave in the White House experiences the burning of Washington, D.C. by the British
in Virginia in 1814 during the War of 1812.

Minahan, John A. *Abigail's Drum*. New York: Pippin Press, 1995.
Based on an actual event during the War of 1812, two young daughters of the local
lighthouse keeper in a Massachusetts town figure out a way to save him and the town
when British soldiers kidnap their father.

# Historical Places to Visit

**Fort McHenry National Monument and Historic Shrine**
East Fort Avenue
Baltimore, Maryland 21230-5393
Visitor information: (410) 962-4290
Three miles southeast of the Baltimore Inner Harbor, this park's visitor center houses
exhibits, a model of the star fort, an electric battle map, and a theater where an orientation
film, "The Defense of Fort McHenry," is shown. Take a self-guided tour of the star fort,
statues, cannons, and restored barracks. This battle site inspired Francis Scott Key to write the
poem, "The Star-Spangled Banner," which became the National Anthem of the United States.

**Fort George**
Niagara National Historic Sites
Box 787, 26 Queen Street
Niagara-on-the-Lake, Ontario L0S IJ0
Canada
Visitor information: (905) 468-4257
Dressed in uniforms of the time period, reenactors perform activities typical to life in and
around the fort just before the start of the War of 1812. Soldiers practice drilling and a fife
and drum corps play music from the time period.

**Fort Mackinac**
P.O. Box 370
Mackinac Island, Michigan 49757
Visitor information: (906) 847-3328 or (231) 436-4100
Constructed by British soldiers during the Revolutionary War, Fort Mackinac served as a
lookout in the Straits of Mackinac. Tour some of the original fort buildings and exhibits of
military life from the War of 1812. Musket demonstrations, cannon firings, and tours by
costumed guides are just some of the many activities taking place at the fort.

# Index